Insights from the Inside:

A Legal Guide for Small Businesses and Content Creators

Tyra Hughley, Esq.

First Edition	October 2016
Editor	Nealy Gihan, Purple Inked LLC
Book Design	Jana Seitzer, GeekGirlDigital.com
Printing	CreateSpace

Legal Disclaimer

Nothing in this book is to be construed as legal advice. This book is meant to be a resource for small business owners and content creators to assist them in ascertaining their legal needs. Every situation or scenario is different, and applicable laws can vary by state, county, etc. Neither Tyra Hughley Smith nor BarrisTourista Publishing is dispensing legal advice via this document. Should you need legal advice, please contact the author of this book directly or an attorney of your choosing. Similarly, this book does not constitute accounting or tax advice. BarrisTourista Publishing recommends hiring a tax consultant or accountant to assess your individual needs.

Additionally, nothing in this e-book, nor any workshop put on by or featuring Tyra Hughley Smith shall constitute the formation of an attorney-client relationship. For the avoidance of doubt, unless you have entered into a formal attorney-client relationship with said attorney, Tyra Hughley Smith does not represent you as counsel nor has such representation been contemplated.

Copyright Notice

Copyright © 2016 by BarrisTourista. All rights reserved.

You are welcome to print a copy of this document for your personal use. Other than that, no part of this publication may be reproduced, stored, or transmitted in any form or by any means, electronic, mechanical, photocopying, recording, scanning, or otherwise, except as permitted under Section 107 or 108 of the 1976 United States Copyright Act, without the prior written permission of the author. Requests to the author and publisher for permission should be addressed to the following email: info@barristourista.com.

Limitation of liability/disclaimer of warranty: While the publisher and author have used their best efforts in preparing this guide and workbook, they make no representations or warranties with respect to the accuracy or completeness of the contents of this document and specifically disclaim any implied warranties of merchantability or fitness for particular purpose. No warranty may be created or extended by sales representatives, promoters, or written sales materials.

The advice and strategies contained herein may not be suitable for your situation. You should consult with a professional where appropriate. Neither the publisher nor author shall be liable for any loss of profit or any other commercial damages, including but not limited to special, incidental, consequential, or other damages.

Contents

	What This Book Covers	5
1	Why You Should Consult an Attorney in Your Business	7
	Section I: Business Formations	9
2	Why You Need a Legal Entities	11
3	Types of Legal Entities	13
4	Steps to Form a Business Entity	17
5	Formalities to Follow to Protect Yourself	21
6	Types of Contracts Small Businesses Need	25
	Section 2: Copyright Law	27
7	Why Everyone Needs to Know Copyright Law	29
8	What Is (and Is Not) Covered By Copyright	31
9	Who Is Protected Under Copyright and for How Long	35
10	Your Rights Under Copyright Law	35
11	What Constitutes a Copyright Infringement	39
12	Why Should I Register My Work with the Copyright Office?	47
13	The "Public Domain": What is it?	55
14	What to Do if Your Work is Infringed Upon	51
15	Fair Use	53
16	How to Protect Your Work	55
17	The Digital Millennium Copyright Act (DMCA)	57
	Copyright Conclusion	59
	Section 3: Trademark Law	61
18	What is a Trademark or Service Mark	63
19	Difference Between Copyright and Trademark	65
20	What Can Be Trademarked	67
21	Three Types of Trademarks You Can Register	71
22	What is a "Classification"	73
23	Rights Afforded to Trademark Owners and What Constitutes an Infringement	75
24	Fees Associated With Trademarks	79
25	Why Should I Register My Trademark	81
26	Process for Getting a Trademark	83
	Conclusion	87

Tyra Hughley, Esq.

What this Book Covers

As a small business owner, there are numerous things you have to tackle. Customer service. Delivering your product/service. Inventory. Scheduling. Managing staff. There are a lot of things you are undoubtedly juggling.

This book is a resource for your legal needs. It is broken down into three sections: Business Formations, Copyright Law, and Trademark Law. These are three areas that every business owner needs to be mindful of in order to ensure he or she doesn't undermine his or her substantive work.

The Business Formations section details different types of legal entities, the protection they offer, and what that means for your business. It covers why you should form a legal business entity and the steps necessary to ensure your business is formed correctly. This section also details the measures you need to take to ensure your continued personal protection in business. And lastly, this chapter lists some crucial contracts that small businesses should have in order to ensure legal protection and make sure their business functions smoothly.

The next section is Copyright Law. Copyright law affects everyone, not just content creators. This section details why this is the case, what is covered under copyright protection, and what your rights are under the law. This section also discusses what constitutes copyright infringement, what to do if you see someone has infringed upon your intellectual property, and how to protect your work.

In addition, this section details how you can avoid being on the receiving end of a cease and desist letter for copyright infringement, and what does and does not constitute a defense to copyright infringement.

The third and final section of this book is Trademark Law. This section details the difference between trademark and copyright law, along with what is protected by trademark law. It also discusses the process of filing a trademark and what you have to do to maintain your trademark ownership.

These areas of law are vast, and there is no way that this book could contain everything. But it is a comprehensive look at the law and provides you with adequate working knowledge of these areas so you can best protect yourself in your day-to-day business dealings. We hope this proves helpful, and, as always, if you have additional questions, you should reach out to legal counsel.

Chapter 1: Why You Should Consult an Attorney in Your Business

I am a firm believer in hiring people to do what they are good at. This is why I don't file my own taxes: I have an accountant for that. This is why I have a web developer. She can do in twenty minutes what would take me two hours. This is why someone should hire you in your area of expertise rather than doing it themselves, right? Exactly.

The same principle applies for your business. You may believe you can do it all, but if you want your business to grow, at some point you have to delegate and outsource work. You are only one person. But it goes beyond that. You need someone to protect you. You need an advocate. Legalities are extremely nuanced and not easily understood by a lay person. That is, after all, why law school is three additional years after undergraduate school (a very expensive three years). Not to mention, attorneys have to take and pass the bar exam in their respective states. This is to ensure (or at the very least attempt to ensure) that qualified and competent attorneys are licensed in order to advocate on behalf of others.

Attorneys are trained to be critical thinkers and to anticipate problems. I can say with confidence that I think of contingencies and scenarios that my clients don't even contemplate. I ask questions that they had not previously thought of when drafting contracts and other legal documents. That is our role: to think of the "what ifs" in order to protect your rights in the best way we know how.

This is especially important for content creators and small businesses. One wrong move can cost you thousands of dollars. And even though hiring an attorney (and similarly an accountant or a consultant or any other professional) is an investment, as I always tell my clients, it is much more expensive to fix a problem on the back end than it is to avoid a problem by having things in writing and handled correctly on the front end.

Content creators—be it writers, photographers, videographers, etc.—have the unique consideration of protecting their intellectual property. Copyright and trademark protection was deemed so important that it (copyright) is mentioned in the United States Constitution. The law to protect your rights, the Copyright Act of 1976, is a federal law, and copyright infringement matters are handled in federal court. It is serious stuff. Even if you think your blog isn't big enough or someone tells you that you should be flattered that they are offering you "exposure," know that you have rights and are entitled to be compensated for your work. Similarly, with respect to trademark law, your business name and its reputation are two of your most important assets. Don't let someone else capitalize and cash in on the work that you have put into building your business.

Above all else, we as attorneys are here to help you. We are here to protect you and your rights. Hiring the right attorney is important, as that person will become an integral part of your team. This book should not substitute your need for an attorney. It is meant to be a resource in helping you know what to look for and what to do in the meantime, and it gives you background knowledge and information so that you can learn (to some extent) how best to protect yourself on a fundamental level.

Section 1: Business Formation

Tyra Hughley, Esq.

Chapter 2: Why You Need a Legal Business Entity

First off, congratulations on starting your own business! Entrepreneurship is a beautiful thing, and you are on the way to taking control of your own destiny.

If you are a small business owner and are reading this e-book, you probably at the very least have thought about forming a business entity for your business if you haven't already done that. But if you are still on the fence, I want to offer three main reasons as to why small business owners should form legal entities beyond sole proprietorship sooner rather than later.

Legal Protection
The biggest reason you should form a business entity for your business is for legal protection of your personal assets and wealth. When you form a legal entity—such as an LLC or a corporation—you are protecting your personal assets from potential legal action. Should a legal situation arise, the opposing party will have to recover from the LLC or the corporation. If you have followed the correct legal procedures, the opposing party will not be able to attack your personal bank account, the bank account of your spouse, nor seize your tangible assets such as your home or car.

This is so important because sometimes legal matters come up, even for the best of business people. Be it a contract dispute or a slip and fall, you want to make sure that one alleged legal misstep doesn't negatively affect your future or your family's stability.

Credibility
There is something to be said for someone who has a formal business that they can refer to their potential customers and clients. It says that you take your business seriously and that you don't consider it to be just a hobby. When dealing with other businesses, it will give you an appearance of professionalism and credibility in your dealings. And that credibility may be the difference between you getting a contract or someone passing you by.

Tax Implications
Disclaimer: I am not a tax attorney nor an accountant. Please consult with a tax attorney or accountant regarding your unique situation.
When you have business expenses, you are able to write them off for tax purposes. That means that you are able to factor in certain expenses in order to either owe less in taxes or obtain a refund come April 15. And when your business is an LLC or a corporation, there is a good chance that the IRS will be less likely to see your business as a "hobby" for tax purposes, especially if you have not been profitable.

As you can see, there are numerous reasons that one should form a legal entity. But if you are going to form a legal entity, you have to follow the correct steps and adhere to the correct formalities in order to make sure you are indeed protected from legal action. The coming chapters discuss the general process for forming a legal entity, along with the corporate formalities one must follow in order to ensure protection.

Chapter 3: Types of Legal Entities

In this section, we will discuss business entities and which may be the best option for your business.

Choosing the type of entity that is best for your company depends on a number of factors. Some of them include tax implications, number of members, type of business, and even what entity types are available in your state. Below is a list of several types of business entities. Bear in mind, your particular state may have restrictions on the type of entity you can form, so always check that factor first and foremost.

- **Corporation**: A corporation is an independent legal entity from its owners, who are called shareholders. The agreement between the owners of a corporation is referred to as the bylaws. There are two common types of corporations: S-Corps and C-Corps. Corporations have the most formalities of all entity types, requiring annual meetings and regular meetings (with whatever frequency as set forth in the bylaws) with minutes kept. Lastly, corporations offer their shareholders a level of protection that shields them from personal liability (provided they follow standard corporate formalities).

- **Limited liability company (LLC)**: LLCs also offer their members protection that shields them from personal liability. LLCs are governed by an operating agreement between the members, and there is no limit on the number of members. An LLC is taxed similarly to a sole proprietorship if it is a single-member LLC or similarly to a partnership if there are multiple members. Another key difference between LLCs and corporations is that LLCs are not required to uphold some of the corporate formalities that a corporation must, such as annual meetings and keeping minutes (though obviously it is recommended that members record the happenings of a meeting for future reference).

- **Sole proprietorship**: A sole proprietorship is a single person business that does not have any corporate formalities, nor does it have to be filed with the state. It is the easiest type of business to start up, because an individual just starts doing business (still following applicable laws). The owner reports all profits and losses on his or her personal tax return. However, this form of business offers you the least amount of legal protection. Because there is no business entity, the sole proprietor is personally liable for all debts and legal action against the business.

- **General partnership**: This is a voluntary agreement between two or more parties to share the profits and losses of a business. Typically, you don't have to file with the state to form a partnership, but obviously you would want to have an agreement between the partners governing the partnership. A general partnership also does not afford much legal protection, and individual partners can be held liable for the actions of another partner.

- **Limited liability partnerships**: While partnerships generally remain personally liable for the debts and lawsuits against the business, a limited liability partnership has some of the protections of an LLC because some or all of the partners have limited liability. Typically, with an LLP, partners are not liable for the other partners' negligence or misconduct. This is a relatively new business entity type, and it is not permitted in all states. But in some states where an LLP is a valid legal entity (such as California, for example), there may be additional restrictions on what types of businesses can classify.

What is not considered a legal business entity:

- **Joint venture**: A joint venture is not a legal entity. It is when two entities (or individuals) join together for a specific project. The extent of the relationship lies only in the particular project that is the subject of the joint-venture agreement, and both parties are usually considered independent contractors with no legal relationship or obligations to each other outside of the terms of the agreement.

- **Fictitious business name**: Having a fictitious business name (or "doing business as" or d/b/a as it is commonly referred to) does not constitute a formal business entity. However, businesses trading under different names can get a d/b/a to legally distinguish the different branches of the business. For example, say you are an informal sole proprietor and your name is Jane Dominguez. You want to call your business "Flowers by Jane;" you can obtain a fictitious business name so that you can legally do business as Flowers by Jane (since your legal name is Jane Dominguez).

S-Corp Versus C-Corp: The Differences

This is a question that many people have when contemplating the type of business they want to form. What is an S-Corp versus a C-Corp? Generally, the difference is in tax treatment. A C-Corp is subject to double taxation, while an S-Corp has one level taxation, and the income is allocated to the shareholders of the corporation on their personal tax returns. But S-Corps are limited to 100 shareholders, and they must all be U.S. citizens or residents. Special forms must be filed to become an S-Corp, but both entities must follow corporate formalities (e.g., annual meetings, etc.).

For more information on the differences between an S-Corp and C-Corp and to confirm this information, consult with a tax attorney or accountant.

Tyra Hughley, Esq.

Chapter 4: Steps to Form a Business Entity

Disclaimer: Every state has different laws, processes, and entities regarding business formation in that state. Additionally, each state may or may not allow different types of business entities within that state. Check your respective state to determine the applicable information for you and your business.

While every state is different, generally speaking, there are a few things you want to do in forming your business entity. Having an attorney assist you with the process is preferable, but below are the general steps for forming your business.

Step #1: Make sure you name is available

After you have determined the type of entity you want to form and have made sure your chosen entity type is available in your state, next up is making sure the name is available. Before you get attached to a name, you will want to do a name availability search. For this, go to your state's entity for business formations (usually the Secretary of State) and do an online name search. Search your name and names that are close or similar to your name and review the results. You may also want to search state trademark registrations as well, along with the Fictitious Business Name registry. But above all else, before you go buying domain names or getting stationary printed, you want to make sure your name is free and clear in your state. Not to mention, you may want to see if the same name is being used widely in other parts of the country as well as in a similar field that may cause consumer confusion.

Step #2: Fill out the Articles of Incorporation or Organization, depending on the entity

The Articles of Incorporation or Organization is the paperwork that needs to be filed usually with the Secretary of State in order to form your legal entity. While the forms usually come with basic filing instructions, you will have to consider substantive factors, such as whether you want to be a member-managed or manager-managed LLC.

The Articles will need to contain the names and information of all of the members of the company in many instances. If you are forming a business entity with multiple individuals or entities, you will want to discuss important aspects of the business prior to forming.

Here are some factors to consider when forming your business:

- Registered Agent: The registered agent will be the person listed online with the business entity information as the contact. In the event of legal action, this will be the person that is served paperwork and the go-to contact. You can also hire a company to be the registered agent for your business. Tip: If you choose an individual member, be sure to have a business address in the state to use as the registered agent's address, so that the person's home address isn't listed on the Internet.

- Member-managed versus manager-managed: A member-managed LLC means that all of the members are responsible for running the operations of the business while in manager-managed LLCs, the members choose a manager to run operations. Having a manager-managed business does not mean that the manager gets to make major decisions, but instead, the manager runs the day-to-day operations of the business within the parameters of the operating agreement. And members can always (and do) set the parameters for the manager in the business operating agreement. It may help to consult with an attorney to see which option is best for you.

Step #3: Submit Articles and extra requirements

Check with your state to find out if there are extra requirements after you submit your Articles (and payment) and they are approved. For example, in California you have two requirements within four months of your Articles being submitted and approved. First, you have to file a Statement of Information, detailing the CEO of the company, any managers, addresses, and the registered agent of the company. This must be filed within 90 days of filing the original Articles. Additionally, in California, the mandatory minimum annual "Franchise Tax" is due by the fifteenth day of the fourth month of the LLC or corporation's existence in the state. Always check to make sure you are complying with additional requirements per your state.

Step #4: Get an EIN

Once you have your corporate entity number, you will want to go to the IRS website and get an EIN (Employer Identification Number). Depending on the entity, it may be free or a minimal cost and takes only minutes to secure. But this will be necessary for the next step, which is opening your business bank account.

Step #5: Open your bank account

In order to open your bank account, you will need your valid and/or stamped Articles and the business EIN. You want to be sure that you set up a separate business account for your business, as will be discussed in the next section on corporate formalities and protecting yourself.

Step #6: Finalize an operating agreement

An operating agreement (or corporate bylaws for a corporation) is a crucial part of any business. It sets forth the rules and methods for various aspects of the business, including capital contributions, debt reimbursements, voting, management, etc. Even if you are a single-member corporation or LLC, you should still have an operating agreement in place. And, in fact, some banks may require it to open a bank account. Not to mention if you are seeking some sort of certification or investors, this will be a crucial document. It should be extremely thorough (the ones I draft for my clients are typically around 30 pages for a standard agreement).

Step #7: Check on annual requirements

Be sure to know and understand the annual requirement of your state in order to keep your business in good standing. As mentioned, in California, you have to file a biennial Statement of Information and submit annual minimum franchise taxes. In Illinois, you must complete an annual report and pay a fee to remain in good standing. Every state is different and has its own requirements. Be sure to be aware of any ongoing obligations so that your business stays active and in good standing with the state.

Can I Register My Business In One State and Do Business In Another?

People ask all the time, "Well, can I form my company in Nevada/Texas/Whatever Inexpensive State even if I am in California?" The answer is yes and no. It will vary by state, but many states have Foreign Corporation status for companies. This means that if you are based in another state but doing substantial business in the more expensive state (e.g., California), then you will have to register your business with California as well and still pay the same franchise taxes as though you were based in California. So in short, you are paying twice: once in the home state and once in California. This will vary from state to state, for sure, so make sure you are not paying twice when you could have just formed in the state in which you are based in the first place.

Chapter 5: Formalities to Follow to Protect Yourself

Business entities such as corporations and limited liability companies offer protection to their owners, but only if the owners adhere to certain requirements and formalities.

Generally, corporations have more requirements than LLCs do. Annual meetings are required. Minutes must be taken. While it is encouraged for notes to be taken at LLC meetings, it is not required. But there are other business formalities that should be taken in order to ensure that owners do not end up being personally liable for liabilities of the company.

Piercing the corporate veil

In corporate law, there is a concept called "piercing the corporate veil." The general idea is that corporations/LLCs shield the owners from liability (hence, the veil). However, the veil can be "pierced," and the owners can be held liable if they act in certain ways regarding the business. Other than failing to follow the corporate formalities listed above, three big offenses are as followed:

- **Commingling funds**: This is a huge one and a quick way to get a court to pierce the veil and find owners of a company personally liable in a legal action. Where there is no real financial separation between a business and its owner, they are often commingling personal and business assets. One example would be paying personal bills from business checking accounts. This is why it is especially important to set up a business banking account once you form your corporation or LLC and use that account only to conduct business. This also applies with other accounts such as PayPal accounts, which many businesses use. Of course, you can still deposit your own money into the business account (which is called a capital contribution) and remove money from the business account to pay owners (which are called dividends or distributions or draws), but you need to make sure to keep detailed books and records of all of these transactions in order to be on the up and up if you do run into a legal situation. It cannot look like you are simply using the corporate bank account as your personal account nor that you are using the corporate structure solely for legal protection or as a shell.

- **Under-capitalization of the business**: Similarly, you have to properly capitalize your business. It is one thing to be operating in the red; that is acceptable. But you cannot be taking out million-dollar loans or contracts and only have a few dollars in the business bank account (and all of the rest of the money in your personal account). Also, when making initial investments, make sure they are reasonable amounts to cover anticipated initial expenses so you don't have to spend directly from your personal account.

- **The owners acted recklessly or fraudulently**: If you are reckless with company funds (beyond reasonable business judgment) or you make huge business deals knowing that you cannot pay the invoices, then creditors may be able to come after the owners directly and pierce the corporate veil. This doesn't mean you cannot make incorrect decisions or investments. This means that you must act reasonably in your position in the company and not defraud owners or lenders, as an extreme example.

The moral of the story is that you must be sure to treat your business like a business, not a hobby or a tax shelter and not just a source of legal protection for bad-faith dealings. If you treat the business like a reputable business and operate it as such, then you will have the protection that an LLC or corporation offers. Otherwise, you may be held personally liable if someone takes legal action against you in court.

Chapter 6:
Types of Contracts Small Businesses Need

Every business needs contracts in order to do business. It is always safe to memorialize the agreement between entities in writing. Write it down! This allows you to avoid future misunderstandings, have recourse if someone acts in bad faith or maliciously, or even have something to refer to if terms are somehow forgotten. As I mentioned, it is always easier to have the proper documentation in order on the front end than it is to fix an error or misunderstanding on the back end (or even worse, in court).

- **Owners agreement**: This agreement is essential. For a corporation, it is the bylaws; for an LLC, it is the operating agreement. For a partnership, be sure to have some sort of partnership agreement between all of the partners.

- **Non-disclosure/confidentiality agreement**: A solid NDA is an essential contract for anyone contemplating doing business with another entity or person. Prior to disclosing your idea or confidential information with an entity or individual you want to form a business relationship with, you should always have an NDA in place. This agreement states that neither party can disclose confidential information of the other party nor can they use such information for their own gain outside of the relationship between the parties. A good NDA helps to protect your ideas, your resources and your connections, even if a business relationship is not formed or even after the relationship ends.

- **Work for hire agreement**: This is also an essential agreement. Did you know if you have someone design your logo, for example, you don't own the copyright in the logo? That is, unless you have a work for hire agreement in place. This will be discussed more in detail in the copyright section of this book, but these should be used for any multitude of creative projects, such as logo design, graphic design, website design, photography, video, etc.

- **Independent contractor agreement**: If you plan to work with others that you do not employ, then you need to have an independent contractor agreement. This agreement states the terms of engagement and also states that you do not employ the individual or entity and that they are an independent contractor. Thus, the contractor is responsible for his or her own taxes, not you as an employer. An independent contractor agreement could also help from a liability standpoint in certain instances. Do note that you still have a duty to oversee people that are working on your behalf (even contractors) and make sure they are adhering to the law with respect to the actions that they do on your behalf.

- **Lease**: This one is self-explanatory. If you are renting space, be sure to have a lease with the landlord. Business and commercial leases are typically quite a bit more complicated than residential leases, so be sure that everything is memorialized in writing.

- **Joint venture agreement**: A joint venture is defined as a commercial enterprise undertaken jointly by two or more parties that otherwise retain their distinct identities. A joint venture agreement is needed when two entities plan to work together on a limited basis on a project. The two entities are not joining, and no partnership is formed, but instead, they are working together for a particular duration or a particular project. Thus, it is best to have an express agreement that states management, ownership expectations, the handling of debts and contributions, and the splitting of profits.

Section 2: Copyright Law

Tyra Hughley, Esq.

Chapter 7:
Why Everyone Needs to Know Copyright Law

You may be thinking, "I am just a normal small business owner. What does this have to do with me?" or, "I'm not a blogger, so I don't need to be worried about copyright law."

You could not be more wrong. Copyright law affects everyone. Does your business have a website? There are copyright law implications. Do you create intellectual property or use other people's work? Copyright implications. Did you create a fancy new logo for your business? Well, you get the point.

The Founding Fathers thought copyright so important that they included it in the United States Constitution. Article I, Section 8 states that Congress shall have the power "To promote the Progress of Science and useful Arts, by securing for limited Times to Authors and Inventors the exclusive Right to their respective Writings and Discoveries." This, dear friends, is the Copyright (and Patent) Clause of the Constitution.

Since that time, Congress has enacted several federal laws to protect the rights of creatives. The Copyright Act of 1976 (with its subsequent amendments) is the primary law governing copyright in the United States. Copyright disputes are adjudicated in federal courts, which have exclusive jurisdiction over copyright matters.

But what does that have to do with you? See above. Our country is built on creativity and innovation, and even the Framers recognized this centuries ago. That is why it is protected by federal law, not just state law. All of your intellectual property is protected. The words on your website are protected. The photographs of your products are protected. And similarly, the photographs and words and music of others are also protected. You could be infringing on someone's copyright and not even know it. But if the owner finds out and comes after you for violating his or her rights, it could end up costing you thousands of dollars. That is why copyright law matters. And that is why it behooves all business owners to know a little something about it before it's too late.

Chapter 8:
What is (and is Not) Covered by Copyright

Let's break down all of the facets of copyright law. This is going to be a long one (with some citations so you can read the applicable sections of the law yourself), so settle in.

What is covered by copyright law?
Section 102 of the Copyright Act lays out the categories of what is covered by copyright. After laying out the language of the law, we will break down the various components.

Copyright protects "original works of authorship fixed in any tangible medium of expression, now known or later developed, from which they can be perceived, reproduced, or otherwise communicated, either directly or with the aid of a machine or device. Works of authorship include the following categories: (1) literary works; (2) musical works, including any accompanying words; (3) dramatic works, including any accompanying music; (4) pantomimes and choreographic works; (5) pictorial, graphic, and sculptural works; (6) motion pictures and other audiovisual works; (7) sound recordings; and (8) architectural works. In no case does copyright protection for an original work of authorship extend to any idea, procedure, process, system, method of operation, concept, principle, or discovery, regardless of the form in which it is described, explained, illustrated, or embodied in such work."

So let's unpack the requirements of copyright law and the key categories of protection.

Original works of authorship: In order to obtain a copyright in for a work, it must be original. This is because, as discussed later in the rights of the copyright holder chapter, a copyright holder has the right to create "derivative works" of the original work.

Some of the categories of works covered by copyright include the following:

- **Literary works**: These are works not including audiovisual works that are "expressed in words, numbers, or other verbal or numerical symbols" in various media, including books, periodicals, manuscripts, film, tapes, recordings, etc.

- **Musical works (including accompanying words)**: This category includes the music, melody, accompaniment, arrangement, lyrics, score, or anything set to music.

- **Dramatic works**: This is just what you would think. This category contains drama, including plays, shorts, etc.

- **Pictorial, graphic works**: This category includes "two-dimensional and three-dimensional works of fine, graphic, and applied art, photographs, prints and art reproductions, maps, globes, charts, diagrams, models, and technical drawings, including architectural plans."

- **Motion pictures and other audiovisual works**: This category captures two areas. Motion pictures are defined in Section 101 as "audiovisual works consisting of a series of related images which, when shown in succession, impart an impression of motion, together with accompanying sounds, if any." Other audiovisual works are "works that consist of a series of related images which are intrinsically intended to be shown by the use of machines, or devices such as projectors, viewers, or electronic equipment, together with accompanying sounds, if any, regardless of the nature of the material objects, such as films or tapes, in which the works are embodied." This is separate from dramatic works, as seen above.

- **Sound recordings**: This is a type of a catchall category that overlaps with other categories, including audiovisual, motion pictures, music, and more. It is defined as "works that result from the fixation of a series of musical, spoken, or other sounds, but not including the sounds accompanying a motion picture or other audiovisual work, regardless of the nature of the material objects, such as disks, tapes, or other phonorecords, in which they are embodied." Thus, you can have a sound recording of a literary work, for example, and that underlying work would constitute a separate copyright.

There are other categories of covered works, but these categories cover most bases. Thus, as long as the work is original and is fixed in a tangible medium or form of expression, the creator owns a copyright in the work.

What is not covered by copyright law?

Not every creative enterprise you envisage is covered by copyright. There are several categories of works that are not covered by copyright. They are as follows:

- Works not fixed in a tangible medium

As you just saw in the Act, copyright law only protects original works of authorship that are "fixed in a tangible medium of expression." (Copyright Act Section 102). Section 101 of the Act defines "fixed" as: "A work is 'fixed' in a tangible medium of expression when its embodiment in a copy or phonorecord, by or under the authority of the author, is sufficiently permanent or stable to permit it to be perceived, reproduced, or otherwise communicated for a period of more than transitory duration. A work consisting of sounds, images, or both, that are being transmitted, is 'fixed' for purposes of this title if a fixation of the work is being made simultaneously with its transmission."

So what does that mean in layman's terms? It means that if someone makes an improvisational speech, for example, and it isn't fixed (written or recorded), it may be free for usage without liability. But if something is recorded or written/transcribed, in some medium or form, it is "fixed" and is subject to and protected by copyright law.

- Ideas or expressions

Simply put, you cannot copyright an idea. You can copyright the expression of the idea fixed in a tangible medium, but the idea itself is not copyrightable. This is why we see the same plot over and over in movies (boy meets girl, girl rejects boy, boy pursues girl, girl falls in love with boy, boy and girl live happily ever after) and other creative works. You can, however, own a copyright in the tangible expression of an idea (words on a page, a treatment, a movie script, etc.). But when a potential client says, "X studio stole my idea," my first question for him or her is "Did they steal a general concept or do you mean they stole your script or treatment?" The latter I can fight; the former is a dead end.

- Works by the U.S. Government

The U.S. Government cannot hold a copyright in its works, including press releases, speeches of federal government officials given in the course of their employment, and other governmental works.

- Words and phrases

Words and phrases, such as your business name, are not copyrightable. They are subject to trademark, which we discuss in the next section. Copyright law also does not protect symbols or trade dress (such as the red and silver signature can of Coca Cola), and those areas are also subject to trademark law. However, if your logo or design contains a certain level of creativity and originality and is not just words, it may be covered by copyright as well as trademark law.

- Works in the public domain

If a work is in the public domain, then copyright law does not cover the work. We will delve more deeply into what constitutes works in the public domain in Chapter 12.

Chapter 9: Who is Protected Under Copyright and for How Long

Copyright law protects the copyright owner. The copyright owner is the person who owns a particular right in copyright. So why didn't I just say that copyright law protects the author? Well, owner and author are not always synonymous. In many instances, the author is the copyright owner, but in some instances, this is not the case.

Authorship: The author is the person who creates the work. In literary works, he or she would be the person who creates and writes the article/story/treatment. In photography, he or she is the person who clicks the shutter. For a musical composition, he or she is the songwriter. If this person doesn't convey his or her rights, then he or she is the copyright owner and receives protection under the Act. If he or she does convey the work, then some entity other than the author is the owner of the copyright of the work. Additionally, the rights afforded under the Act may pass down to the heirs of the author.

Initial ownership of a copyright vests in the original author. And it is immediate. You don't have to do anything additional. So as soon as you write that article or that book or as soon as you snap the shutter on your iPhone, you have a right in the copyright of that literary work or photograph. No additional steps are required. The work is created, and you own it. What you do with it from that point on, however, can make all of the difference in the world.

Joint works: A joint work is one that is created by two or more authors. The intention between the authors is that the work will become merged into inseparable parts of a whole. A common example of a joint work is two songwriters who work together to create the lyrics and melody of a song.

So what does this mean for you as a joint owner? This means that you have every right to exploit the work in any way you see fit (except transferring the other person's ownership, as you will see below). You can license the song, you can allow a reprint of the book, you can license the photograph all without the consent of the other joint owner. Your one obligation: you must account to the joint owner(s) for their share of profits earned from use of the copyrighted work.

Transfer of ownership: So can you just transfer away your rights by saying, "Yeah, you can use my song," or "Sure, you can reprint my article in your publication"? The short answer is no.

The Copyright Act seeks to protect copyright holders, and, surely, the folks drafting the laws realized that people could be bamboozled into giving away their rights. This is why Section 201(d) of the Copyright Act provides that a copyright can be transferred or bequeathed by will, but it must be done in writing. "A transfer of copyright ownership, other than by operation of law, is not valid unless an instrument of conveyance, or a note or memorandum of the transfer, is in writing and signed by the owner of the rights conveyed or such owner's duly authorized agent." So you cannot just tell someone they can use your work and lose all rights in your intellectual property.

But what you have more likely done when conveying your works verbally is created a revocable, nonexclusive license to use the work. This can be revoked or rescinded at any time, unless the license is in writing (and then the terms of the agreement will govern).

This is why it is very important to be careful about signing any document regarding the implications on your intellectual property. If it is not clear that you retain any and all rights or if the document makes the license irrevocable, you will want to consult a lawyer to ensure that you understand your rights. Similarly, if the license is exclusive in nature, you will want to consult an attorney, so as to understand whether you have any rights as the copyright holder to shop or use your own work.

> ### Works Made for Hire
> So what happens when you hire someone to create your work on your behalf? Who owns the work? If you hire someone to create your logo, for example, then that person owns the rights in the copyright of the image. Even if it is understood that they are creating it on your behalf as work for hire, the author still owns the work. That is why you need a written work for hire agreement. You will remember that the only way to convey a copyright is in writing. So drafting a work for hire agreement conveying the work from the designer to you, the business owner, is the only way to legally convey the ownership of the work.

How long does my copyright last?

How long your copyright lasts depends on when the work was created. Any work that was published in the United States before 1923 no longer has copyright protection and is in the public domain. For works published after 1923 but before 1978, the length of the copyright is 95 years from the date of publication. If a work was created after January 1, 1978, or if the work was created but not published until after that date, then the life of the copyright is the life of the artist plus 70 years.

What is "publication?"

In order to know when your copyright expires, you have to first know the date of publication. This, quite frankly, is the toughest portion of the Copyright Act to decipher given the recent changes in technology. Section 101 of the Copyright Act defines publication as "the distribution of copies or phonorecords of a work to the public by sale or other transfer of ownership, or by rental, lease, or lending. The offering to distribute copies or phonorecords to a group of persons for purposes of further distribution, public performance, or public display, constitutes publication. A public performance or display of a work does not of itself constitute publication."

So why is this so tricky? It seems like as soon as you make the work available for sale or licensing, the work is published. Short answer: social media and the Internet. With the advent of Facebook and the like, the line between when something is published and when it isn't has become blurred. By placing something on one's blog or online gallery, for example, does this constitute making something available for licensing? What if you didn't intend to license something but someone contacts you about licensing? What constitutes a "distribution" in the context of social media? Generally, if you contact people about licensing or make the work available for sale, it is published. If not, it isn't published (but that doesn't mean you don't hold a copyright in the work).

Chapter 10: Your Rights Under Copyright Law

Copyright owners have exclusive rights as set forth by the Copyright Act. Generally, you have the right to copy your work (hence the term "copyright").

But what does that mean exactly? Section 106 details the exclusive rights of copyright holders under the law.
Subject to other provisions of the Act, "the owner of copyright under this title has the exclusive rights to do and to authorize any of the following: (1) to reproduce the copyrighted work in copies or phonorecords; (2) to prepare derivative works based upon the copyrighted work; (3) to distribute copies or phonorecords of the copyrighted work to the public by sale or other transfer of ownership, or by rental, lease, or lending; (4) in the case of literary, musical, dramatic, and choreographic works, pantomimes, and motion pictures and other audiovisual works, to perform the copyrighted work publicly; (5) in the case of literary, musical, dramatic, and choreographic works, pantomimes, and pictorial, graphic, or sculptural works, including the individual images of a motion picture or other audiovisual work, to display the copyrighted work publicly; and (6) in the case of sound recordings, to perform the copyrighted work publicly by means of a digital audio transmission."

The right to reproduce means the right to copy or facilitate the copying of your work. The right to perform publicly is just what it sounds like: you have a right to perform your work or allow others to do so in a public space. The right to display your work means that you have the right to make your work available to the public in any way, including on the Internet. You can put your photos in a gallery, create a YouTube channel for video, put your pictures on Facebook or Instagram, post articles on your blog, and post words or compositions on other mediums. All of that falls within your exclusive rights as a copyright holder. You get to determine how and when that happens and the terms under which those actions happen. So when someone says that if you want to preserve your rights you shouldn't place your work on the Internet, that is blaming the victim of the infringement, instead of placing the blame where it should be: on the infringer. You have every right to display your work in any way you see fit; infringers have an obligation not to infringe upon your rights.

What is a Derivative Work

Copyright owners are also allowed the exclusive right to create "derivative works." Section 101 of the Copyright Act defines derivative works as "a work based upon one or more preexisting works, such as a translation, musical arrangement, dramatization, fictionalization, motion picture version, sound recording, art reproduction, abridgment, condensation, or any other form in which a work may be recast, transformed, or adapted. A work consisting of editorial revisions, annotations, elaborations, or other modifications, which, as a whole, represent an original work of authorship, is a 'derivative work'." So think of a derivative work as a remix, a sequel to a movie, or a second edition of a book. Anytime you take one of your original works and make a newer version of the work, you have created a derivative work that you have exclusive copyright rights in.

As the exclusive holder of these rights, that doesn't mean you have to do everything yourself. It simply means that you get to determine how works will be performed or displayed or copied. Copyright owners alone have the right to determine whether they want to license works or how they want to profit from their intellectual property.

Chapter 11:
What Constitutes a Copyright Infringement

Copyright infringement occurs when the rights of the lawful copyright owner are violated. Section 501 of the Copyright Act states: "Anyone who violates any of the exclusive rights of the copyright owner as provided by sections 106 through 122 . . . is an infringer of the copyright or right of the author, as the case may be."

Copyright infringement is much like a strict liability offense, which means that it doesn't matter if you do not mean to infringe or if you infringed unintentionally. If you use a work without the permission of the lawful copyright owner, you have committed an infringement and are liable for damages. Additionally, despite what many will argue, removing the image upon notification of the infringement does not totally fix the problem. Removing the image merely eliminates future damages; it does not alleviate past damages for infringement.

Does an infringer have to pay damages even if he or she didn't mean to infringe or didn't know the work was subject to copyright?
Yes, an infringer can be liable for damages even if he or she knew nothing about copyright laws. This is where the age old adage "ignorance of the law is not a defense" comes into play. The infringer's knowledge, however, may factor into how much is owed for an infringement.

How do you determine how much is owed for a copyright infringement?

The Copyright Act clearly lays out the different types of damages for copyright infringement in Section 504 of the Act.

- **Actual damages**: "The copyright owner is entitled to recover the actual damages suffered by him or her as a result of the infringement, and any profits of the infringer that are attributable to the infringement and are not taken into account in computing the actual damages. In establishing the infringer's profits, the copyright owner is required to present proof only of the infringer's gross revenue, and the infringer is required to prove his or her deductible expenses and the elements of profit attributable to factors other than the copyrighted work." You will note that actual damages do not just include the profits of the infringer; it also includes the damages of the copyright holder. This may come in the form of lost sales or quantifiable usurped business opportunities, or more commonly, a licensing fee for the work.

- **Statutory damages**: What do statutory damages mean? Think mandatory minimum sentences for criminal law. If an infringement occurs and if the work is timely registered (see also the next chapter on why you should register your work), then the copyright owner is entitled to receive damages for the infringement within the statutory range. "The copyright owner may elect, at any time before final judgment is rendered, to recover, instead of actual damages and profits, an award of statutory damages for all infringements involved in the action, with respect to any one work … in a sum of not less than $750 or more than $30,000 as the court considers just. For the purposes of this subsection, all the parts of a compilation or derivative work constitute one work." The reason for awarding statutory damages has different facets. First, it is meant to further protect copyright owners who take the extra step of registering their work with the Copyright Office. Perhaps you wouldn't have charged $750 to license the work; this allows you to obtain a higher amount that low licensing fees. Second, it is meant as a punishment or as a deterrent to copyright infringers. Where your damages fall in the scheme of things depends on other factors, as detailed below. And remember, with statutory damages, copyright owners have the right to elect which damages they prefer. If actual damages are higher, you can clearly elect that option.

Courts will consider and weigh several factors in determining how much to award in statutory damages if a matter proceeds to court. However, even if the matter is not in court, these are factors that can be taken into consideration in negotiations.

- **How egregious or widespread was the usage**: If the usage was particularly egregious or widespread, the copyright owner may be entitled to more in statutory damages.

- **The nature of the infringer**: The type of infringer can play a role in how much will be awarded in statutory damages as well. Tiny, non-tech-savvy, mom-and-pop shops may not be forced to pay as much in damages for a small usage. But a huge media company that should know better may have to pay more in damages (because the media company reasonably knows or should know better than to infringe on the rights of others) and probably has some measure of safeguards in place, which adds to the argument that it knew better.

- **Whether the infringer avails him or herself of copyright law**: This ties in with the last point. For example, a media company not only should know better, but it likely fiercely protects its own copyrighted work. So if you know enough about copyright to protect yourself, then surely you should know to respect the rights of others.

- **Patterns of behavior**: If the person or entity is a chronic copyright infringer or perhaps is infringing on more than one work of the copyright holder, then this shows a pattern of bad behavior that can be taken into account.

Willful infringements

Willful infringements take regular copyright infringements up a notch. The Copyright Act states: "In a case where the copyright owner sustains the burden of proving, and the court finds, that infringement was committed willfully, the court in its discretion may increase the award of statutory damages to a sum of not more than $150,000." So instead of the normal threshold of $30,000 per infringement, the threshold amount can be raised to five times that amount as a max per infringement.

But the copyright holder has the burden of proving that an infringement was willful. It is a difficult threshold to clear, but there are some factors that courts have used in assessing willfulness.

- **The work had clear attribution on it**: If say a video or a photograph has a watermark and the infringer posts the video or photograph with the watermark, courts can use that factor in finding the infringement to be willful. The infringer had actual notice on the work itself or even immediately adjacent to the work and posted the work with the notice, so the infringer cannot say that he or she did not know the source of the work. Not to mention, the infringer had plenty of ability to ask the permission of the copyright owner.

- **Failing to remove a work within a reasonable time of being notified**: If you are notified that you have infringed upon someone's copyrighted work, remove the work immediately at the very least out of an abundance of caution. This is not an admission of guilt. Instead, this is ensuring that you don't get hit with additional liability. If an infringer fails to remove a work in a reasonable amount of time and continues to infringe, then that infringement is willful. The infringer had actual notice and chose to ignore it and continue to infringe. Courts are much more likely to find for willfulness in this instance.

> ### What is Innocent Infringement
> Many infringers will mistake the term "innocent infringement" with unintentional infringement. They use this argument to lower the minimum statutory amount from $750 per infringement to $200 per infringement. But unintentional and innocent infringements are not the same thing. In fact, innocent infringement is actually a relatively challenging legal bar to surpass. Courts have stated that in order for an innocent infringement to occur, the infringer must show not only that he or she thought had the authorization to use the copyright owner's photograph, but also that such belief was reasonable (Case: National Football v. Primetime 24 Joint Venture). Thus, this standard is challenging because the person cannot assert that he or she did not know who the copyright owner was or that the work was subject to copyright, because if that was the case, how could he or she have believed that he or she had the lawful rights to use the work from the copyright holder?

Willful infringement is tough to prove, but if an infringer acts in an egregious manner, then that can mean enhanced damages if you are eligible for statutory damages.

What if I attribute?

Attributing the source of the work without obtaining permission does not alleviate copyright infringement liability. In fact, it tends to show that the infringement may have been willful because the infringer knew that the work was owned by someone else, knew who that person or entity was, and still chose not to obtain permission prior to infringing on the work. While some copyright holders may be fine with mere attribution, others may rightfully deem that it is not enough. Attribution alone will not save the day.

Other ways to commit an infringement

There are other ways that a copyright infringement can occur, rather than just displaying or copying the work of another. Here are two examples.

- **Exceeding the terms of the license**: You can commit a copyright infringement even if you have a lawful license to use the work. This happens if you exceed the terms of the license. Let's say you license a work for web usage only and then you print it out on brochures or t-shirts. Then you have committed an infringement and can be held liable for damages. Or let's say you license a work for a set duration of time, such as a year term, but you exceed that time frame. Same thing, this is considered a copyright infringement.

- **Distribute to others**: One of the exclusive rights of a copyright owner is the right to copy or distribute the work. If an infringer distributes the work for unauthorized use by others, that infringer has committed both a primary and secondary infringement. The primary infringement occurs in the distribution. But then if the other entity has no idea that it is using the work unlawfully and it displays the work, for example, then the infringer also facilitated that infringement as well.

Chapter 12: Why Should I Register My Work with the Copyright Office?

The word "copyright" is very often used incorrectly. It is used as verb rather than a noun. Many people mistakenly believe that if they have not "copyrighted" their work, they do not have any rights. This is totally incorrect. What they mean to say is that if they haven't "registered" their copyrighted work with the Copyright Office, they don't have any rights (by registering, I mean filing an application for copyright to get a certificate of copyright ownership). This is also untrue. But you should still make it a habit to register your work.

Here's why you should register your copyrighted work with the Copyright Office:

- You are entitled to increased damages for an infringement.

If you do not register your work timely and it is infringed upon, you are still entitled to damages but only actual damages. Actual damages are limited to (1) the profits of the infringer and (2) the actual loss suffered by the copyright owner. Typically, if an infringement is on the Internet, for example, there may not be any profits. But the licensing fee for the work that you would have charged would be the actual losses. And the licensing fees may not be more than a few hundred dollars.

If, on the other hand, you register your work timely with the Copyright Office, you will be entitled to a range of statutory damages. At minimum, you are entitled to $750 per infringement, ranging up to $30,000 per infringement. Where your damages fall on that scale will be determined by several factors, including the egregiousness of the infringement. To register timely, you must register your work with the Copyright Office before the infringement occurs or within three months of publishing the work.

- You can obtain a willfulness enhancement.

In addition to regular statutory damages, if your work is registered timely, you may also be entitled to a willfulness enhancement if the infringement is deemed to be willful. Courts have defined willfulness as the infringer having actual knowledge that it was infringing on the copyright owner's rights or it should have known and acted recklessly with regard to those rights. Courts have also found that if you have identifying information on the work, such information supports a finding for willfulness (because the infringer had actual notice that someone was asserting copyright ownership of the work). You can only get a willfulness enhancement if you meet the requirements to receive statutory damages.

- You can easily demonstrate proof of ownership

Oftentimes, the first thing an infringer asks me when confronted with a claim of copyright infringement is for the registration information on the work. A registration is extremely strong proof of ownership of the work, and infringers (rightfully so) will want this type of evidence so that they know they are not getting bamboozled into potentially paying thousands of dollars to someone who doesn't even own the work. It is much easier to deal with an infringer with that proof already in hand than it is to prove that you own the work via other means.

- You can file suit for copyright infringement and obtain attorneys fees.

Lastly, you should register your work so that you have any and all options available to you if needed. Under U.S. law, you cannot file a lawsuit for copyright infringement until the work is registered with the Copyright Office. If the work is already registered prior to needing to file a lawsuit, you can avoid rush fees, which are several hundred dollars for an expedited registration filing. Additionally, if you have registered the work prior timely, then you may also be entitled to recover your attorneys fees and costs of litigation under Section 505 of the Copyright Act.

Registering your works is not a terribly difficult process and can be done online. The Copyright Office will want a "specimen" or a number of copies of the work to examine. And the fee is about $55 per registration. And, in many instances, you don't have to file each of your works separately; you can file them as a compilation or collection.

Where Do I Go To Register My Work?

To register your work, you visit www.copyright.gov. Please do note that obtaining an ISBN or other classification number, or doing a "poor man's copyright" does not substitute for filing an application for copyright registration with the Copyright Office.

Tyra Hughley, Esq.

Chapter 13: The "Public Domain": What is it?

When people infringe on others' copyrights, one of the most frequently used and typical excuses I hear is "the photo was in the public domain." This is, nine times of out ten, totally incorrect.

So what is the public domain? Works that are in the public domain are works that are free to be used by anyone without permission and with no liability. All works published in the United States before 1923 are in the public domain. Governmental works are also in the public domain.

Works also enter the public domain after the expiration of the term of the copyright, as detailed in Chapter 9. The only other way for a work to enter the public domain is if the copyright owner places the work in the public domain. To do this, the author would have to put a statement similar to this statement: "This work is in the public domain and is free for use by anyone for any reason." But be advised: This statement has to come from the copyright holder, and as the person who wants to use the work, it is your duty to ensure that is the case. The burden is on you.

What is NOT the Public Domain?
The few examples listed above cover the vast majority of works that are in the public domain. What is not in the public domain (but I hear it a lot from infringers) are the following:

- **Pictures/works found on Google**: Just because you found it on Google does not make something in the public domain. Let me repeat that: Google does not equal public domain.

Google is a search engine/aggregator. It finds most instances of a work on the web. Just because something appears in a Google search does not mean you can use it free of charge. The example I give infringers is that you can find music or New York Times articles on Google. Does that mean you can steal them for your business use? In fact, in Google Images, Google actually states that images may be subject to copyright. Listen to them and assume that the images are subject to copyright.

- **Pictures/words/works on another website**: Same thing here. Just because a picture or image or song or other work appears on another website does not mean it is in the public domain. Someone could have lawfully licensed that work and as part of the license, they do not have to provide attribution. Or, on the contrast, someone could have stolen that work, and by taking it, you are stealing it from someone who never even had lawful rights to the work. That will not absolve you of your liability for copyright infringement.

- **Pictures/graphics/works on a "free download" site**: Many people visit websites touting free graphics and pictures, believing the pictures to be in the public domain. This is also not the case. And as a side note: Be very careful about what sites you download these images from. Often times they do not have the rights to license the works and/or they are less than reputable. Remember, these are free sites, often with little to no contact information, and they may or may not be based overseas, leaving you little recourse if an infringement is alleged. Buyer beware.

Chapter 14:
What to Do if Your Work is Infringed Upon

When they find out their work has been infringed upon, most people want to immediately blast the individual or entity about the copyright infringement on social media. However, this may not be the best approach.

The first thing you should do is collect evidence of the infringement. Take a number of screenshots showing the URL and the infringement on the web page so you have evidence. Also, be sure to check social media and do the same. You will want this evidence in the event you have to pursue legal action. Once you notify the entity, then it is going to remove the infringing work (as it should), and your evidence will be gone.

The next step should be to contact your attorney. When an infringement occurs, you are entitled to damages. But depending on the type of infringement, you may decide you don't want to pursue legal action. That is fine, but your attorney can still send a cease and desist letter on your behalf, citing the relevant copyright law and demanding that the infringing work be promptly removed (and requesting damages for the infringement).

The key is to be sure that you collect your evidence before you send takedown notices or reach out via social media. The evidence is the most important thing, and if you end up having to prove the infringement, the evidence is all you will have to show that the infringement actually occurred.

Above all else, you will want to try to resolve the matter amicably via settlement before filing suit. An attorney can help you with doing this. However, if the matter is unable to be reasonably settled, you have three years from the discovery of the infringement (in most circuits) to file a lawsuit. Three years is the statute of limitations for copyright infringement claims.

Chapter 15: Fair Use

Often times, people will argue that their usage of your work is a "fair use." They will argue this as though they did not commit a copyright infringement.

Fair use does not imply that a copyright infringement didn't occur. Quite the contrary. It is a defense to copyright infringement. That means that by asserting fair use, an infringer is acknowledging that he or she has committed a copyright infringement but is arguing that, for one reason or another, the infringement is excused.

The Copyright Act states that "the fair use of a copyrighted work, including such use by reproduction in copies or phonorecords or by any other means specified by that section, for purposes such as criticism, comment, news reporting, teaching (including multiple copies for classroom use), scholarship, or research, is not an infringement of copyright." The Act goes on to further lay out four factors used in assessing fair use. They are as follows: "(1) the purpose and character of the use, including whether such use is of a commercial nature or is for nonprofit educational purposes; (2) the nature of the copyrighted work; (3) the amount and substantiality of the portion used in relation to the copyrighted work as a whole; and (4) the effect of the use upon the potential market for or value of the copyrighted work."

The Supreme Court has also weighed in on the matter in the 1994 landmark case Campbell v. Acuff-Rose Music. In this case, the Court determined that these factors are a sliding scale and, for something like a parody, the infringer is actually allowed to use quite a bit of the copyrighted work.

When it comes down to it, a court has to make a complete determination on fair use. But generally, the fair use argument is most widely accepted and valid in the context of newsworthy journalism usage (think breaking news) and educational settings for schools and colleges. When I say educational settings that does not mean anything used to educate the public. Simply writing an informative article or blog post does not make your usage of someone's work a fair use. For example, law firms often have informative blog posts on their websites. But these websites are to promote the law firm and are commercial in nature. Thus, this probably would not classify as a fair use primarily for an educational usage. However, if a work is used in a classroom setting, it will be afforded much greater protection.

Even having a nonprofit organization does not definitively mean usage of a work is a fair use. It is a factor in determining fair use, but it is not the determining factor. The courts will look at the type of usage as well. And even for journalists, some courts have found that just because some work or photograph or video may be newsworthy doesn't necessarily mean that journalistic outlets don't have to license the works ahead of time. That is simply not the case.

Chapter 16: How to Protect Your Work

Bad news: even if you take all the precautions in the world, there is a chance your work will still be infringed upon. It's a bummer. But there are some ways you can protect yourself move than usual, and perhaps if someone does infringe, you will at least be entitled to more damages.

Here are a few ways to protect your work:

- **Provide clear attribution/watermarks**: Providing clear attribution that the work is under your authorship and subject to copyright can at least combat someone saying he or she had no idea that the work was copyrighted. Place a copyright notice at the bottom of your web page. Include a byline with your work. Watermark photographs and images that you created. At the very least, infringers are put on notice and cannot claim an innocent infringement. But do note that even if you do not, for example, watermark your photographs, you are still afforded the same protection under the Copyright Act. But taking these measures might entitle you to more in damages as some courts have found that having identifying information on a work makes the infringement willful.

- **Disable right-click saves and/or copy and paste**: You can add technological countermeasures to your website to protect your intellectual property. For example, on my website, you cannot copy and paste text from my blog. Additionally, you cannot right click and save an image from my website. These are technological countermeasures to prevent infringements. If someone wanted to infringe on a photograph from my website, they would have to take a screenshot of the page and save that screenshot. By doing that—by circumventing my technological protections—an infringer will have actually violated the Digital Millennium Copyright Act (which we discuss in more depth in the next chapter), and as the author, I would be entitled to additional damages and recourse because of that intentional behavior.

- **Police your work**: Be sure to police your work. Every so often, enter a block of text from your website into Google and see what comes up. Or for images, Google has a reverse image search where you can upload, and it shows you all instances of that image (or close to it) on the Internet. There are also companies that will do this for a fee, I believe. Policing your work will not prevent an infringement, but at the very least, it will allow you to be aware of infringements and handle them promptly.

- **Register your work with the Copyright Office**: By registering your work with the Copyright Office you have a presumption of ownership of the work. This will allow you, as a last resort (always try to settle the matter first with the help of your attorney), to file a lawsuit for copyright infringement. You can only file a lawsuit for copyright infringement if the work is registered with the Copyright Office prior to filing suit. Otherwise, your case will be dismissed, and you may end up paying for the attorneys fees of the infringer!

Chapter 17:
The Digital Millennium Copyright Act (DMCA)

Given the increase in technology, Congress sought to address the widespread infringements that occurred with the assistance of technology (and in spite of it) by enacting the Digital Millennium Copyright Act (DMCA) in 1998.

What does the DMCA do for you? The act states that if someone intentionally circumvents technological protections of copyrighted works or if someone removes copyright ownership identifying information, he or she has committed a DMCA violation and are liable for increased damages, with a minimum threshold of $2,500 per violation. This means if someone takes a screenshot because he or she cannot right-click save your image or copy and paste your words or if someone intentionally crops of your watermark or removes your metadata from your work that identifies your copyright ownership from a photograph with the intent to conceal such ownership, he or she has committed a DMCA violation.

The DMCA is meant to help people who take additional measures to protect their work. It is harder to prove, but if you have a valid DMCA claim, you are entitled to damages ranging from $2,500 to $25,000 per violation, in addition to the damages you are entitled to for the actual copyright infringement.

Tyra Hughley, Esq.

Copyright Conclusion

So as you can see, copyright law affects everyone, not just content providers. It affects any business owner in some way or another. And it is important to make sure that not only are you protecting your intellectual property but that you are respecting the rights of others. If you have questions about your unique situation, be sure to contact a knowledgeable copyright attorney who can help you with your particular issue.

Tyra Hughley, Esq.

Section 3: Trademark Law

Tyra Hughley, Esq.

Chapter 18: What is a Trademark or Service Mark

Welcome to the trademark section of this e-book. You made it this far, and now your first question of this section may be "What exactly is a trademark?"

Generally speaking, a trademark (noting that I will use the term trademark in this book as encompassing both trademarks and service marks) is a symbol or word(s) or combination of words and symbols that a company uses to identify itself and its brand in the marketplace. It is the mark under which a company trades (see how that works?). It is meant to identify and distinguish the source of goods of one company from another. A trademark can be established by usage and by legally registering the trademark with the United States Patent and Trademark Office (USPTO).

The two primary types of trademarks are trademarks and service marks. The USPTO defines trademarks as marks that are "used by their owners to identify goods, that is, physical commodities, which may be natural, manufactured, or produced, and which are sold or otherwise transported or distributed via interstate commerce." Service marks, on the other hand, are "used by their owners to identify services, that is, intangible activities, which are performed by one person for the benefit of a person or persons other than himself, either for pay or otherwise."

So why does your business need to have its trademarks protected? Because your trademark represents your company. It represents your goodwill and reputation. By not protecting your business name and the products it represents, you are allowing someone to come in and not only trade on your name but trade on your reputation. If you have built a reputation for high-quality standards for your products, then you don't want someone to trade on your name with inferior products and bring down your reputation. There is a reason that the Ritz Carlton doesn't allow Motel 6 to open hotels using its name. Policing your trademark protects your business and its reputation.

> ### What is the Difference Between Goods and Services?
> Knowing the distinction between goods and services is an integral part in registering your mark and obtaining federal protection. The Trademark Office states: "Goods are products, such as bicycles or candles. Services are activities performed for the benefit of someone else, such as bicycle rental services or catering." A business may perform both goods and services and can list both on an application, but it is important to know the distinction. For example, a company that sells shirts is providing goods; a company that does shirt screen printing for customers is providing a service. That is the distinction between goods and services.

Chapter 19:
Difference Between Copyright and Trademark

One of the most common questions about trademarks is what is the difference between a trademark and a copyright? In simple terms, a copyright protects literary and artistic types of works, while a trademark protects things associated with a brand, like its name or logo or trade dress. This is why you cannot obtain a copyright in a business name. But note that you may be able to obtain both a copyright and trademark in a logo if it is a unique and distinct drawing, for example.

Generally speaking, you should think of copyrightable items as the things that a company produces and trademarks as the company's identification itself. It does not have to be limited to just the name. It can be a slogan or even a symbol. Everyone associates "Just Do It" with Nike; in the same way, many remember hearing that "the best part of waking up is Folgers in your cup." There are many ways to create brand identity through words, symbols, sounds, or logos.

What is Trade Dress

Trade dress can also be protected by trademark law. It a legal term that refers to something regarding the appearance of the product. According to the USPTO: "Trade dress originally included only the packaging or 'dressing' of a product, but in recent years has been expanded to encompass the design of a product. It is usually defined as the 'total image and overall appearance' of a product, or the totality of the elements, and 'may include features such as size, shape, color or color combinations, texture, graphics.' (Case: Two Pesos, Inc. v. Taco Cabana, Inc.)." So what does that mean? Think of a Coke can as an easy example. Pepsi could not just create a can of its soda using the red and silver can with the distinct script that Coca Cola uses but instead say Pepsi on the can. That would cause brand confusion and would be a trademark infringement, because although the can design itself is not a mark, it would likely constitute trade dress.

Chapter 20: What Can Be Trademarked

As mentioned, your trademark ties in closely with your brand. Thus, any identifying marks that allow the public to recognize your brand are subject to trademark.

There are requirements for registering a trademark with the USPTO. Each application is evaluated by an examining attorney to ensure that it is unique and distinct enough and does not infringe upon the rights of another trademark.

There are various categories that can receive trademark protection. It is not just words and logos but also other identifying marks that can be registered. Above are some details about trade dress, which is protected under design marks. And here are a number of things that can be trademarked:

- **Words**: Words that are either made up or already existing can form a trademark. If you are applying for a word mark, it shouldn't need a logo in order to be considered sufficiently distinct to be registered. The mark cannot be merely descriptive or generic in nature.

- **Graphical signs such as logos**: A graphical sign can also be registered as a trademark. But a logo or graphical mark does not have to just be a symbol of some sort; it can also include words as well. Often times, it can be easier to get a trademark for a graphical mark because of the distinctness of the symbol. But you still have to ensure that it is distinct and doesn't infringe upon others' marks.

- **Sounds**: Sound marks are less common in the United States, but they can be done. Note that the sound must be very distinctive, and it can also likely be copyrighted. Some examples of famous sound marks are the "Roaring Lion" of MGM or the Harlem Globetrotter music.

- **Shapes and colors**: Shapes and colors can also be trademarked. The shape must be a recognizable one that allows the public to identify with the brand. A couple of examples of this may be the Nike "Swoosh" (although that is also a logo) or the shape of the Coca Cola bottle. As to a color trademark, the most widely known color trademark is "Tiffany Blue," which is a registered trademark of Tiffany & Co., the jewelry company. Another color mark is the red color on the bottom of shoes, which is distinctly registered to Christian Louboutin.

What cannot be trademarked?

But not every mark can be trademarked. The USPTO has criteria on what can receive federal trademark protection. Here are a couple of categories that cannot be trademarked:

- **Generic words**: You cannot obtain a trademark in generic words that describe a whole class of goods or services. For example, if your mark is "Bob's Blinging Shirts," you may be able to get a trademark in the whole name, but you will have to disclaim the exclusive use to the word shirt. That means that while someone may not be able to use your entire mark, he or she can certainly use the word shirt in his or her mark as well.

- **Marks that have been abandoned**: The requirement for continued trademark protection is use in commerce. Thus, if a business abandons the mark, usually through nonuse of the mark, the trademark protection ceases. There also must be sufficient evidence that the owner no longer intends to use the mark in the marketplace.

- **Confusingly similar marks**: The USPTO will not register a mark for federal protection if the issuance of the mark is likely to cause confusion amongst consumers. This "likelihood of confusion" standard is discussed in a later chapter.

- **Someone else's name**: You cannot obtain a trademark in someone else's name without that person's express consent. This is why the names of celebrities or celebrities' children's names can be at least somewhat protected. And you only may be able to get a trademark in your own name. Typically, you cannot register what is considered "merely a surname" with the Trademark Office and be afforded federal protection. This is especially true if, say, you share the same name as a celebrity business. The name must acquire a secondary meaning as a brand, not just as a person's name.

Distinctiveness requirement for obtaining a trademark

The more distinctive a mark, the more likely the owner is to have trademark protection. Distinctiveness is the most important factor in a trademark, as it goes to the very crux of the reason for trademark. The mark has to be distinct enough to allow consumers to identify the source from which the goods are coming and allow them to recognize the brand.

According to the Trademark Manual of Examining Procedure: "With regard to trademark significance, matter may be categorized along a continuum, ranging from marks that are highly distinctive to matter that is a generic name for the goods or services. The degree of distinctiveness—or, on the other hand, descriptiveness—of a designation can be determined only by considering it in relation to the specific goods or services. Remington Products, Inc. v. N. Am. Philips Corp." The manual goes on to say:

> "At one extreme are marks that, when used in relation to the goods or services, are completely arbitrary or fanciful. Next on the continuum are suggestive marks, followed by merely descriptive matter. Finally, generic terms for the goods or services are at the opposite end of the continuum from arbitrary or fanciful

marks. ... Fanciful, arbitrary, and suggestive marks, often referred to as 'inherently distinctive' marks, are registrable on the Principal Register without proof of acquired distinctiveness. Marks that are merely descriptive of the goods or services may not be registered on the Principal Register absent a showing of acquired distinctiveness under 15 U.S.C. §1052(f). ... Matter that is generic for the goods or services is not registrable on either the Principal or the Supplemental Register under any circumstances."

Thus, the more fanciful or arbitrary your mark is, the more likely you are to be able to obtain federal trademark registration.

How Do I Create My Trademark

In the United States, you don't create a trademark by simply registering names with the USPTO. You create a trademark by using the mark in commerce. These "use-based" rights are common law rights in trademark, but they are based on a certain area. That area is usually local in nature, because it is based on the area in which your mark is used or recognized as your brand. So unless you have a national or international brand, if you don't register your trademark, you are likely only protected in as far as your mark would be recognized. This may make it more challenging to enforce your rights in a widespread area.

Chapter 21:
Three Types of Trademarks You Can Register

When you are filing for trademark protection, one major consideration is what type of mark do you want to file. The three types of marks you can register are (1) standard character marks, (2) stylized/design format mark, or (3) a sound mark.

- **Standard character mark**: A standard character mark "should be used to register word(s), letter(s), number(s) or any combination thereof, without claim to any particular font style, size, or color, and absent any design element." This type of mark is when you are just trademarking the words with no design elements, including color. This is the broadest form of trademark protection, because you are applying for protection of the words itself, not their depiction. This means that you can use them in any font, color, logo, style, and you still have broad protection in the words themselves; the presentation of the words is irrelevant for this type of registration.

- **Stylized/Design mark**: "The stylized/design format, on the other hand, is appropriate if you wish to register word(s) and/or letter(s) having a particular stylized appearance, a mark consisting of a design element, or a combination of stylized wording and a design." Once the registration is issued, your mark will be assigned a design code. A stylized mark is words in a particular font and/or color, and a design mark is a logo or drawing. This type of mark can include both words and a drawing, but it cannot contain a standard character mark. That means that if your name is Bob's Blinging Shirts and you only get a design mark, then someone can, theoretically, take those same words, create a different design, and have a mark in that logo if it is not similar to yours, because you have not formally protected the words themselves. This type of mark is helpful if you have a very distinct logo, but may not be as helpful if you ever decide to change the logo, as only the submitted design will have federal protection.

- **Sound Mark**: This mark is pretty self-explanatory. Here, you are seeking to trademark a specific sound.

Actual Use Versus "Intent to Use" Applications

When you are registering your trademark, there are two types of "basis" for filing: 1A registration for actual use and 1B registration for "intent to use." The USPTO clarifies: "If you have already used your mark in commerce, you may file under the 'use in commerce' basis. If you have not yet used your mark, but intend to use it in the future, you must file under the 'intent to use' basis. This means you have a bona fide intent to use the mark in commerce; that is, you have more than just an idea but are less than market ready." Note that if you file an intent to use registration, you have to file additional forms and pay an additional fee every six months.

Chapter 22: What is a "Classification"

Classifications are the way that the USPTO classifies goods, services, and the scope of registrations. When you receive a federal trademark registration, it is per classification not widespread protection for any type of usage spanning all categories.

Classes are broken down according to the Acceptable Identification of Goods and Services Manual. This provides a searchable database of all classes. Depending on what your trademark covers, you may have to register in multiple classes (this is usually the case) in order to protect yourself for all uses of the mark.

The classes are broken down into various categories. For example, shirts and clothing are in Classification 25. But Classification 25 also includes other related items such as hats, sweatshirts, and more. You want to make sure you cover all areas in a particular class that the mark is used on.

Say you have an online clothing store. You will want protection for all of the types of apparel that the mark is used on. But what about your store itself? Well, an online store is in a different class than apparel. That is where the multiple classifications come in, as you will have to file an application for both of those classes. And let's say you have recently expanded to include jewelry; that, too, is another class. So you could easily have three different classes just to protect your one store that sells clothing and jewelry.

Tyra Hughley, Esq.

Chapter 23: Rights Afforded to Trademark Owners and What Constitutes an Infringement

Trademark, like copyright, is an exclusive right in favor of the rights holder. This right gives the holder of the trademark the right to stop others from trading on the mark. This right, however, is limited to use in commerce, because the whole aim of trademark law is to prevent consumer confusion with regard to goods and services for sale and in use in commerce.

The usage of a mark depends on the classifications that the mark is registered in. Trademark law does not just protect you for the goods or services that you have, but also anticipates the fact that businesses grow and expand into similar areas. This is the purpose of the classifications: to group similar goods and services together so as to avoid a likelihood of confusion in related business fields.

If someone uses your mark on the same products
If you sell shirts and someone creates a shirt and uses the same identifying words or logo, this is a trademark infringement. Think counterfeiting in this instance. The impact on the consumer is clear: they think they are getting (usually) luxury goods made to a certain quality, and they are actually getting cheap knockoffs. This not only hurts the consumer but also the brand's name and reputation.

Likelihood of confusion
If someone uses a mark in perhaps a closely related area or perhaps uses a mark that is not exactly your mark but similar, the standard for evaluating these types of trademark infringement claims is

whether it causes a "likelihood of confusion" for the consumer.

According to the U.S. Patent and Trademark Office, a "likelihood of confusion" is the most common reason to refuse a trademark registration. The USPTO states that a likelihood of confusion exists when both "(1) the marks are similar, and (2) the goods and/or services of the parties are related such that consumers would mistakenly believe they come from the same source."

This means consumers may mistakenly buy the wrong product, thinking they are buying something from another company. The goods or services need to be related, per the USPTO's information on trademark filings and basics as follows:

> "Even if two marks are found to be confusingly similar, a likelihood of confusion will exist only if the goods and/or services upon which or in connection with the marks are used are, in fact, related. Whether the goods and/or services are related is determined by considering the commercial relationship between the goods and/or services identified in the application with those identified in the registration or earlier-filed application. To find relatedness between goods and/or services, the goods and/or services do not have to be identical. It is sufficient that they are related in such a manner that consumers are likely to assume (mistakenly) that they come from a common source. The issue is not whether the actual goods and/or services are likely to be confused but, rather, whether a likelihood of confusion would exist as to the source of the goods and/or services."

Here are a couple of examples to illustrate this. The previous example re: Pepsi selling its products in a red and silver can with the same fanciful script as a Coke can but instead writing Pepsi on the can. There is a good chance that consumers, not paying close attention, would grab that can thinking they were getting Coke because of the unique trademark and trade dress of Coca Cola. This is a high likelihood of confusion.

But it doesn't even have to be the same product. Trademark

protection also helps with related products. For example, if you sell shirts, it is not unreasonable for a consumer to think that you would start to sell hats, so someone shouldn't be able to trade off of the same or similar name on hats and other apparel, for example, because customers would think that it is the same brand and a reasonable extension of that brand and purchase the wrong products unknowingly.

Dilution of the brand

Additionally, if two marks are similar, and the usage of one mark would tarnish or damage the original brand, the courts may find that the registered mark is protected. As mentioned previously, trademark protects the holder's reputation, and trading on his or her name in any way that could damage the reputation of a brand may be able to be enjoined and considered trademark infringement. A perfect real-life example was Victoria's Secret's trademark infringement case against a sex toy shop in Kentucky called Victor's Secret (see what he did there?). Not only would this possibly cause a likelihood of infringement, but also the court found that this was a dilution of Victoria's Secret's mark. It was not unreasonable for Victoria's Secret to be concerned that associating a sex toy shop with its brand would cause a dilution of brand. The court agreed, found in Victoria's Secret's favor, and the shop now operates under a different name.

Remedies if a trademark infringement occurs

If a trademark infringement occurs and a court finds that an infringement occurred, the most important thing is that the infringer will have to stop using the mark in commerce and infringing on your rights. You may also be entitled to damages for the trademark infringement, as the infringer will have to hand over any profits he or she made by selling the infringing products. If the products are goods and there is some remaining inventory, the trademark holder can seize those products or order them destroyed.

Trademark rights are strong rights for the trademark holder. Provided that the mark is being used in commerce and the mark is policed, the holder of the rights has the exclusive right in the mark and the right to adjudicate against any mark that comes close to his or her mark in order to protect the business, its profits, and its reputation.

Chapter 24: Fees Associated with Trademarks

The bad news: Registering a trademark is not cheap. It can actually get quite expensive. The good news: Once you have a registration and your business is using the mark, the registration lasts for as long as the mark is in use.

The United States Patent and Trademark Office currently charges between $225-$325 per classification, depending on the type of application method you use. Yes, you read that right (and the fees actually decreased last year from the previous year). Thus, if your mark is being used in a few classifications, you will have to pay the $225-$325 for each classification.

So Why Should You Get a Search Done Professionally?

When filing a trademark, I highly recommend hiring an attorney to assist you. While an attorney cannot guarantee your mark will issue, we can certainly help the situation. Part of the reason to hire an attorney is because that attorney will be doing a comprehensive, "knockout" trademark search and will be analyzing the results. A knockout search examines all uses of the mark in any area of the country and also comes up with a listing of similar marks that may cause problems. An attorney can not only help you with a search but also help you with analyzing the results. Why is this so important? Because the USPTO fees are nonrefundable, even if your mark does not issue. I repeat, even if you do not end up obtaining the trademark registration, you will not get your money back. Again, we as attorneys cannot guarantee results, but we help give you a better chance that your money will not go to waste (not to mention we act as a liaison between the examining attorney and you when a question or concern arises).

Additionally, those fees are for each type of mark. So if you decide to do a word mark and also a logo or picture mark, it is $225-$325 for each of those types of marks multiplied by the number of classifications. You can see how quickly these fees add up.

Chapter 25: Why Should I Register My Trademark

Similar to copyright law, registering a federal trademark is not required by law, but it does enhance your rights. Here are several reasons why registering your trademarks for federal protection is a good idea:

- **Legal presumption of ownership**: When you receive a trademark registration, it is a strong presumption of legal ownership. A USPTO examining attorney reviewed your application and evaluated extensively the mark to make sure there was no likelihood for confusion with other marks before issuing the registration. Thus, by virtue of having that registration, you have an extremely strong presumption of legal ownership and the right to use the mark in the context of the goods and services covered in the registration.

- **Putting the public on notice of ownership**: Registering your trademark inherently, through the entire process, puts the public on notice of your assertion of rights in the mark. As soon as the application is filed, it is in the trademark search system with the USPTO and is searchable. During the process of registration, there is a 30-day period wherein the mark is published for opposition with the public. Thus, the act of registration is important for public awareness.

- **Protection from counterfeit goods**: When you register a mark with the USPTO, you are able to also record the registration with the U.S. Customs and Border Protection Agency so that they can look out for and can prevent the importation of counterfeit goods.

- **Ability to file a lawsuit for trademark infringement**: Just like with copyright law, you cannot file a lawsuit for trademark infringement unless the mark is registered with the USPTO.

> ### Can I Use the TM or ® Symbols?
> Using the ™ for your trademark, or a similar SM symbol (for service marks), is available any time you are asserting trademark ownership. By using the marks, you are telling the public that you are adopting these marks in specific connection with your business or brand. Contrary to what many say, you do not have to have registered the marks nor even started the registration process to include the trademark or service mark superscripts. However, if you wish to use the ® symbol, your mark must be formally registered with the US Patent and Trademark Office.

Chapter 26: Process for Getting a Trademark

In case you didn't know, filing a trademark is an extremely long process. It takes anywhere from nine months to a year, provided that major issues don't arise. The upside is that as soon as you file the mark and submit your fees the application is visible in the USPTO's trademark search system. Here is the entire process and timetable:

Step 1: Fill out the application
After you have done a search and done your legal due diligence, you will fill out the application. At that point, once the fees are paid, your application becomes visible to the public. Again, I recommend hiring an attorney before you get started.

Step 2: The three-month wait
That's right, after your application is filed, there is typically about a three-month wait before your application is even assigned to the examining attorney and reviewed due to administrative delay.

Step 3: The USPTO reviews the application
This is when an examining attorney with the USPTO is assigned to your application and will review the file and determine whether a federal registration is permitted. This takes approximately one month. If the application is acceptable, it will be published (see below).

Step 4: The USPTO issues an "office action"
This almost always happens. When the USPTO issues an office action, it is inquiring about something in your registration. The USPTO could need a better specimen or perhaps it needs you to

disclaim usage of a word or it could have other more substantive questions. The applicant must respond within six months of receiving the office action in order to have the mark not be considered abandoned.

Step 5: The applicant responds timely

If you respond within the six-month period, the examining attorney will typically take one to two months to review your response and ensure it is acceptable. If the response is acceptable, the mark will be published. If not, the examining attorney will issue another office action that must be resolved.

Step 6: The mark is published

Once the mark is published, you are not in the clear yet. This does not mean that your trademark registration will issue. By law, the USPTO has to publish every potential mark in the Official Gazette and allow for public opposition of the registration of the mark. So one month after your mark is approved for publication, it will appear in the Official Gazette for a 30-day opposition period. If there is opposition, the person can file an objection, and no further action will be taken on the mark until the opposition is resolved. If no opposition occurs, then you move on to registration.

Step 7: The mark registers

If there is no opposition, approximately three months after the publication in the Official Gazette, the USPTO issues a registration. If there was an opposition, once the Trademark Trial and Appeal Board clears the opposition, the mark registers. About a month later, you will receive a registration certificate.

Step 8: Maintenance of the mark

In order to maintain a "live" mark, you need to do more than just use it. Between the five- and six-year marks of receiving the registration, you must file a Declaration of Use. And every ten years, you have to file similar documents to maintain your registration.

If you meet those requirements, your mark will live on as long as it is in use. But as you can see, it is a long, tedious process that involves a lot of waiting periods. Throughout the whole process, you can check on the status of the application online on the USPTO's website.

Tyra Hughley, Esq.

Conclusion

So, there you have it: essentials of business formation, copyright law, and trademark law in a (relatively) compact guide. This is obviously not all there is to know (there are huge textbooks on these topics), but this is a great guide to get you going. The key is for you to understand the importance of protecting yourself in these areas and to know your rights so that you can indeed protect yourself.

I hope this e-book has been a great resource for you in your endeavor to cover yourself legally. While it is best not to go at it alone (hire a lawyer, for goodness sakes), this will give you a starting point from which to grow your business. Having the proper framework will allow you to minimize your risk and flourish your business with less worries of legal action or headache. And that's what it is all about: making running a business easier for small business owners.

Tyra Hughley, Esq.